HOWDY DO
ME AND **YOU**

Getting-Along Activities for You and Your Young Child

by Linda Allison and Martha Weston

Little, Brown and Company

Boston   New York   Toronto   London

The authors thank the moms, dads, aunts, uncles, teachers, librarians, and kids who generously shared their ideas, stories, and experience for this book.

A special thanks to Tracy Williams, Ethel Seiderman, and the kids and staff at the Fairfax–San Anselmo Children's Center, Anna Berger, Theresa Hawkin, Lissa Rovetch, Marilyn Wronsky, Louise Robinson, Robert Tomlinson, Ruth Young, and Lucy Young.

A very special thanks to Patricia Monighan Nourot, Ph.D., Professor of Early Childhood Education at Sonoma State University, for guiding the content and adding her ideas, humor, and expert review.

Hearts and flowers to William Wells for adding a dad's point of view, graphic problem-solving, inspired words, general counsel, and support.

The Brown Paper Preschool books are edited and prepared for publication at The Yolla Bolly Press, Covelo, California, under the supervision of James and Carolyn Robertson. Production: Renee Menge. Composition by Wilsted & Taylor, Oakland.

**Library of Congress
Cataloging-in-Publication Data**

Allison, Linda.
 Howdy do me and you : getting-along activities for you and your young child / Linda Allison and Martha Weston. — 1st ed.
  p. cm. — (A Brown paper preschool book)
  Includes index.
  ISBN 0-316-03466-5
  1. Preschool children. 2. Social learning.
3. Parent and child. 4. Creative activities and seat work. I. Weston, Martha. II. Title.
III. Series: Allison, Linda. Brown paper preschool book.
HQ774.5.A45 1996
303.3′2 — dc20   94-47634

Printed in Hong Kong

FIRST EDITION

10 9 8 7 6 5 4 3 2 1

IM

Published simultaneously in Canada by Little, Brown & Company (Canada) Limited

★ CONTENTS ★

SHARING, CARING, GETTING ALONG

CELEBRATING IT ALL

INDEX

★ ABOUT THIS BOOK ★

When we asked a bevy of parents what they most wanted their young ones to know, they didn't answer math or reading. They said cooperation, confidence, self-reliance, empathy, and being able to talk about feelings.

This kind of learning can be classified as social studies. We call it getting-along-in-the-world skills. Whatever you call it, social learning may be the most important learning your kid will ever do.

Social learning is about developing a positive self-image. From this core a child builds confidence, acceptance, and perseverance.

It's about being able to communicate feelings. A child needs to develop a language for the full range of human emotions, as well as skills for coping with them.

It's about sharing, caring, and respecting others. It's learning to accept differences in people and enjoying the diversity of many cultures.

It's learning about work, family, and the neighborhood. It's learning about tradition and celebration. It's knowing what's safe and what's not. It's learning how to navigate in a large and confusing world . . . and what to do when you're lost.

So when do you, Busy Adult, have the time to cover this vast territory with your young one? You already do. Whenever you and your child open the family photo album, sit down to a holiday meal, look in the mirror, shop, walk, or talk about how to solve a problem, you are teaching your child.

This book is simply a collection of fun, breezy, easy activities that enlarges and focuses the path of social learning you and your child are already on. While skills like reading and math can give a child a head start in life, a good set of social skills can mean the difference between surviving and thriving.

Children begin forming a picture of who they are at a very early age. This is a very important picture, because the many decisions that a child makes about who he is and what he can do will become part of the picture he will carry with him for his whole life.

A child builds her picture of "me" in many ways:

There is the physical me. What I look like. My size. How I sound.

There is the doing me. I can swim. I can put on my shoes. I can draw. I can make the kitty purr.

The thinking me. I can read stop signs. I can write my name. I know my street number. I can beat my mom at a game of Concentration.

The feeling me. I feel that other people like and accept me. I have a good friend. My sister makes me mad. My mom loves me. I feel loved and lovable.

Before your child is able to see himself, he will see himself mirrored in your eyes. In many ways you are your child's world. Your view will become incorporated into his. You need to reflect an

accurate picture of your child and the world. Don't confuse him with a tiny version of yourself or with the child you wish you had.

Self-esteem comes from feeling valued and from receiving accurate feedback and genuine praise. When your kid says, "I hate you," don't respond with "You don't mean that." Reflect the truth. "Yes, sometimes you hate me." Your child needs to be heard and to be acknowledged for who she is. Your accurate mirroring and encouragement will help your child form a positive picture of herself. It is the best gift you will ever be able to give her.

★ ME MASK ★

How am I like other people? How am I different? These are basic questions that a young child asks. What if I had a mustache? Green hair? Three eyes? These "Me Masks" encourage kids to observe their own features, then change them for fun.

I see a shiny me!

I like my freckles. I'm making lots more.

Now I gots a mustache!

It's a funny me!

You will need:
a clear plastic soda bottle (liter size)
scissors
markers
glue
yarn, stickers, colored paper

Have Your Child Really Look at His Face.
Ask, "How is your face different from mine? What makes your hair special? Your eyes? Do you have dimples? Freckles? What shade of brown, pink, or tan is your skin?" Compare.

1. Cut the basic mask shape for your child. Start near the center; it's easier.

2. Have your child hold up the mask to his face to mark the nose. Cut out a hole for breathing.

3. Try it on. What do you see? **Decorating hints**: Glue on yarn or paper. Use sticky dots or strips of colored tape to change the face.

★ MIRROR ME ★

Seeing themselves (and being encouraged to like what they see) helps kids develop strong self-images. Fooling around with mirrors and playing with their own reflections allows kids to see many sides of themselves.

MIRROR, MIRROR ON THE WALL

Give your child a strong, safe mirror to play with. (Almost anything that is shiny makes a mirror.) Consider hanging a collection of mirrors low on your child's wall. Just be sure the breakable ones are securely fastened.

SELDOM-SEEN ME

People have many seldom-seen parts. Ask your child to use mirrors to see:

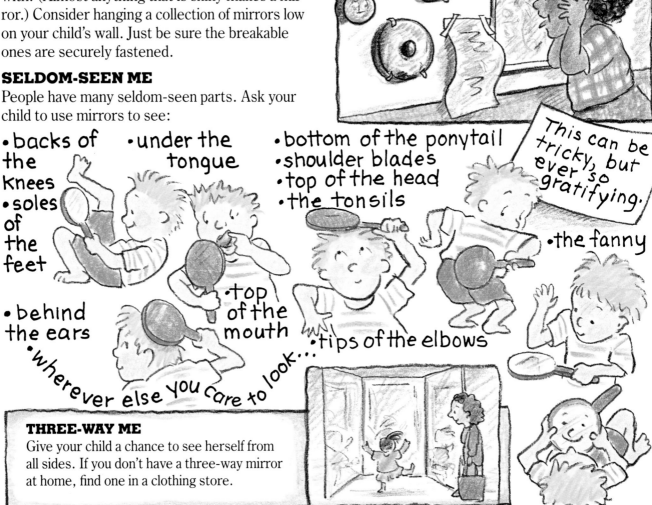

- backs of the knees
- soles of the feet
- behind the ears

- under the tongue
- top of the mouth

- bottom of the ponytail
- shoulder blades
- top of the head
- the tonsils

- tips of the elbows

- the fanny

This can be tricky, but ever so gratifying.

- wherever else you care to look...

THREE-WAY ME
Give your child a chance to see herself from all sides. If you don't have a three-way mirror at home, find one in a clothing store.

★ BIG ME ★

This is a kid classic that is fun no matter how many times you do it. After tracing each other, try tracing your kitty, dog, or any other family member who will take this activity lying down. Hang the full-size drawings in the hall for a family portrait gallery.

You will need:
large sheets of paper or newspaper
tape
markers or crayons
poster paint
scissors

1. Tape together sheets of paper to make a surface big enough to lie down on.
2. Arrange the body. (No wiggling, please!)
3. Trace around the body with a fat felt marker or crayon.
4. Invite your child to draw, color, or paint on the tracing.
5. Cut out the figure and hang it up.

Talk About the Parts. "Hey, Andy, can you find your neck? How about your fingers?" Name and label the parts, then let your child "read" the parts to you.

Trace the Whole Family. Who is smallest? Tallest? How are they alike? What's different? A collection of these drawings over time makes a lovely record of how your child has grown.

★ LOOK-AT-ME BOOKS ★

Kids love looking at pictures of themselves, both as babies and, now, as "big kids." Turn those baby photos into a book, and invite your child to write the story line. This book is bound to be one of your child's favorites for a long time.

Make the Book. Find a small photo album. Or make one from sturdy cardboard:
1. Cut as many sheets as you have photos.
2. Punch each sheet with two holes.
3. Snap the pages together with rings from the stationery store.

WRITE THE STORY

1. Pick out some baby photos. (Photocopies are fine.)

2. Glue them one to a page. Leave room for a caption.

3. Together with your child, write the story. Begin each line, "When I was a baby, I could _____, but now I can _____."

4. Let your child tell how to fill in the blanks.

When I was a baby, I could crawl, but now I can run and jump!

Write down what your child has to say.

5. Read the story to your child. Then let her "read" it to you.

When I was a baby, I sucked my thumb, but now I chew gum.

Other ideas for stories:
• Mica Takes a Bath
• Kia at the Beach
• Dominic's Birthday

★ ALIKE AND DIFFERENT ★

"Mommy, something's wrong with that man's arm," your child blurts out in a loud voice. You can die of embarrassment or take it in stride. When you treat your kid's comments in an open, accepting way, you're teaching your kid to respond to life's differences in the same way.

Like and Not Alike. Little kids spot differences in a flash. Elderly people, disabled people, homeless people—the unfamiliar is often scary for kids (and sometimes for us). Dealing with fear is a skill. Some hints:

1. Find out what your kid is thinking. "What do you notice about that lady?"
2. Respond in a matter-of-fact way. "Right, she has two canes."
3. Clarify and reassure. Explain what's going on and why it's OK, if you can. "Canes are a big help if it's hard to walk."

Handicap Props. Play is a child's way of working out life. Consider providing some helper devices for your child's play. Explain how people have different abilities and how these devices can help.

- earphone hearing aid
- eye patch
- glasses
- foam neck brace
- crutches (kid-size from a thrift shop)

People Are Many Colors. Acknowledge and celebrate the differences in people, and your child will, too. You and your child can take a trip through a magazine and cut swatches of skin colors. How many colors can you find? Do any match your skin color? Observe closely. (Skin tones in different parts of the body will vary.) Compare the people in your family. Try a hair survey next.

Fool around with people colors. Crayons are now sold in packs featuring a wide range of skin tones. Can you find a color that matches the back of your hand?

★ MEASURE ME ★

"I can't believe how much you've grown!" Children suspect adults are making this up. Numbers don't mean much to little ones, but they understand differences. Here are some simple ways to show your child how she has grown and changed. It's also a great introduction to the skill of measuring.

Measuring Door. Even hard-to-impress teenagers find this age-old custom a constant source of wonder.

1. Pick a handy doorway. Mark the heights of everyone in the family with a sharp pencil.
2. Record the date by each mark.
3. Add to the record when the occasion arises—birthdays, when cousins visit, or when someone is feeling especially tall. Make it an extended family game by adding aunts, uncles, friends, and foes.

Shoe Size. Surely you saved your baby's first shoes. Invite your kid to compare them to her current sneakers. Let her hold them on a sheet of paper while you trace their outline. Cut them out and hang them up. Even the size difference of last year's shoes can be astonishing.

So Short. Cut a length of string showing your child's birth length and another showing his current height. Talk about the difference. (Your child's birth certificate or baby book will have some other interesting numbers to compare.)

So Long. Cut strips of paper or strings to show the height of each family member. Mix them up. Can you guess who's who? Label them with names or photos and the date. Now hang them. Then put them away to marvel at in a few years.

Squirt Shirts. Lay your kid's baby shirt on top of your kid's current T-shirt. What's the same? What's different?

Family is the place little ones learn how to see themselves and to see themselves in relation to others. Family is the place where kids figure out who they're like . . . and who they're not like. Family is the first place where kids develop social skills, but their emerging social awareness doesn't happen all at once.

Babies begin life as the center of the universe. Their first task is to figure out where they stop and the rest of the world begins. They can't see themselves, but they can see others.

Around age one, children show a growing awareness of self. By two and a half or three, they begin to develop the notion that some people look the same and others look different. They explore this perception in preschool years, and gradually the knowledge of same and different extends to feelings and ideas.

Around four, you might notice your child picking up a pretend phone and holding a two-sided conversation. Or your kid acting out a daring rescue, playing both the superhero and the helpless victim. At this stage, your child is learning to think in multiple perspectives.

Baby Doll is sad 'cause Bump Bear took all the cookies.

By five or six, a child will begin to develop a sense of how perspectives differ—Kim finishes the cookies that Inez was saving for later.

By seven or eight, a child will be able to hold several viewpoints in his mind simultaneously. This allows him to see a situation from many sides. This is the age when true compromise becomes possible.

At this stage, your kid will probably lose that wonderful, unself-conscious enthusiasm for everything that makes young kids such fun. It goes with your kid's developing ability to step back and see himself from a distance. The good news is that your new self-conscious kid will be a lot better at family give-and-take.

★ FAMILY FACES ★

Brothers, sisters, mom, dad, grandparents, uncles, aunts, and cousins—a whole confusing crowd of people is called a family. Introduce your child to their faces with a portrait gallery for the fridge. Then have some fun sorting out the faces.

The Family Faces. Glue snapshots or photocopies of family members onto juice can lids. Glue magnets on the back of the lids. Stick them on the fridge.

Don't expect little ones to grasp the relationships, but talking about family can give a child a sense of belonging. While you are busy in the kitchen ask: "Who is the smallest?" "Can you find the tallest?"

juice can lid

Glue a magnet on the back.

Glue a photo on the front.

Who's the oldest?

Can you pick out all the girls?

All this family lives together.

Family Tree. Start the tree with your child on the bottom. Put brothers and sisters alongside. Next row: mom, dad. Next row: grandparents. Older kids might want to add in uncles, aunts, and cousins. Do this with family faces, or draw a family tree on a sheet of paper.

★ FAMILY PHOTOS ★

Looking at the family album can be both absorbing and boring for little kids, who mostly want to know "Where am I?" Perusing pictures can help your child see how she fits in to the family whole. There are many ways to look.

Tiny Albums. Kids love to see themselves, so let your child have fun by creating some special little photo albums where he is the star.

Any Theme Will Do. Zoo day. When I was three. Rex gets a bath. Uncle Lon.

Here's me! And Daddy!

Fold some paper in half.

Write a title.

Staple.

Glue or tape photos.

See, Clem? This is before you was our dog.

Yes, Aunt Nell uses a wheelchair.

Why don't *they* have wheelchairs?

Differences. The best place to develop tolerance for diversity is within the family. As you cruise through the family album (or life), treat differences in looks, abilities, age, and styles as just that: differences. Acknowledge them in a straightforward way, but try not to make one way of being better or worse. Just different.
Yes, Uncle Ralph is missing some hair. Zette has spots. They are called freckles. Billie has braces to make his teeth straight. Yes, Raja is dark. His skin has more melanin.

Who Nose? Make a viewer by cutting a small window in a 4 × 6–inch card. As you thumb through the family album, use the card to reveal only parts of photos. Guess whose eyes? Whose funny hat? How did you know this was Al's foot?

I know! That's a monster's hat!

A PHOTO SERIES

Some of the most evocative photos are shots of people standing in the same spot as the years go by. The changes are fascinating. Some families take the same shot by the Christmas tree or gathered around the Thanksgiving turkey. To avoid adding to the holiday confusion, plan a photo session each year at a calmer time: summer by the swing or Jim's half birthday or the first snow day.

Giant sighted near camp!

DANCING IN THE FOG

Sally! Wake up!

FAMILY TALES

Family photos naturally evoke stories from your past or Auntie Em's past. Don't hold back. It's a wonderful way to pass on history and practice the art of storytelling. Make a tape of your conversation. Let your child play it while he views the album.

Tell the story about Daddy and Rex getting mud on Aunt Bea's tea party.

Throwaways. The pictures you'd never send Grandma are suddenly treasures if they come with a funny story. Put those awful snapshots together in a book. Write a zany story to describe them.

Blurry: The wind was really blowing.
Red eyes: Laura was getting no sleep.
Finger over the lens: Aliens arrived.
Washed out: Gene forgot his vitamins.

★ PICTURE THE FAMILY ★

Drawing and talking are wonderful ways to find out how your child feels about her family and her place in it. A child will often say more about what she is feeling while she draws. Plus it's a fine record of her changing ideas.

1. Invite your child to draw members of the family, including herself.
2. When the drawing is done, ask your child to describe what's in the picture.
3. Write it down on the picture. (Always ask permission before you do this.)
4. Invite her to describe each person and what he or she is doing. Talk about size, hair color, eyes, and other details. Do they all wear glasses? Is that a smear or a wart on Aunt Annie's nose? How are they alike? Are they glad or mad?

Steps. It's estimated that more than half of all Americans will live in a stepfamily situation sometime during their lives. Blended families are normal. It is also normal for a young child to confuse her relatives, even in small families. Spare her the confusing details, and welcome anyone she chooses to add to her picture of family, including the family fish.

★ FAVORITE CARDS ★

Little ones love to sort. This activity allows kids to see that everyone sorts differently and that it's perfectly OK to have a different opinion.

You will need:
a stack of magazines
scissors
3×5–inch cards
a glue stick

ANIMAL CARDS

Favorite Cards
1. Thumb through some magazines. Pull out pictures of foods (or whatever topic your child fancies, such as cars or toys).
2. Cut out ten to twenty pictures small enough to fit on the cards. (Kids will need help cutting.)
3. Glue the pictures onto the cards. Label each card, if you like.

Empathy is the ability to see the world from another person's viewpoint. Tolerance is knowing it's OK to have a different view. For small children, the first step is to learn that there are other viewpoints. To develop tolerant children, welcome their opinions, even when they don't agree with yours. This simple sorting game is a way to begin to introduce your child to these concepts.

★TO PLAY★

Make two piles — foods you like and foods you don't like.

I like apples.

I no like peas.

FOOD CARDS

So Gramma likes red best, and I like blue best, and your favorite is yellow.

And Max can't decide his best.

Now try sorting from most favorite to least favorite.

▲ Take turns. Talk about the differences of opinion.

TOYS CARDS

Taking a trip to the market, watching a road being built, talking to the butcher, driving to the dump, walking on the beach, going to a ball game—all are ways to expand your child's understanding of the world.

But don't be surprised if after a dump run you find your kid playing "dump the junk" on the back steps. It's natural for children to imitate just about everything. It's a young child's way of assimilating information and images and assembling them into a mental map of how the world works.

The capacity to represent images from her experience in her mind is a major milestone in a child's mental development.

Role-playing lets your child step back and forth between pretend roles and his real self. By the time he is four or five, he can transform his iden-tity easily and play with ideas in both the real world and fantasy realms. This provides an important component in his developing stable sense of self.

But won't he get stuck in a fantasy world? a worried parent asks. One teacher we know explains it this way: "It's like stairs. If you want your kid to be safe on stairs, do you remove all stairs from your house? No. You let him practice. Practice is how a kid learns how to travel up and down stairs." Fantasy play is how children explore their world by crossing the boundaries between real and pretend, until they become experts at planning, thinking, and imagining.

It is important to provide your child with many real-world excursions so he can have rich experiences from which to create both real and fantasy worlds of her own.

★ NEIGHBORHOOD EXCURSIONS ★

Pets, people, plants, and playgrounds—walking through your neighborhood is your child's best introduction to the world. Go out, walk, talk, and have a ball.

There are many ways to discover your neighborhood. One is to simply let your child take the lead and follow along as she spots an astounding number of things you never noticed. Or take a theme walk:

·COUNTING WALK·
Take a window walk. How many can we count?

Five red cars!

How many pets live on our street? How many red cars? How many monkey bars?

Good job! We'll have lots of marks to follow.

·COLOR WALK·
Let your child pick a color. Ok, today is yellow day. Let's go out and see just how many yellows we can find.

·CHALK WALK·
Make marks along the way. Take the same walk tomorrow. Follow yesterday's chalk trail. Is it still there?

· DOT WALK ·
Take stickers along. Place them along the way. Count as you go. Follow the dots tomorrow. Can you find them all?

·FINDING WALK·
A red leaf, a bottle cap, something with a number on it—make a list of things to collect while you are out.

Another bottle cap!

Add the wild and crazy. You might not find a pink pig, but it doesn't hurt to look.

Hello Walk. "Hello, Cummeskys. Hello, mean dog. Hello, Mr. Wilson. Hello, Jane and stupid little brother Max." Practice saying hello to the houses, even when nobody is there to talk back. It's a good way to learn the neighbors' names.

Say Hello. Communicating is a basic skill. Show your child how to acknowledge the people he knows in the neighborhood. If the challenge of greeting someone is too difficult for your child, how is he going to manage to speak up if something sticky comes up in an interaction?

But what if you choose not to greet a stranger? That's OK. Kids need to know how to handle all kinds of situations. If your child asks, "Mommy, why didn't you say hi?," explain why you decided not to.

There are some very good reasons for your child to know the neighbors: for safety, for a sense of community, and for a chance to practice social skills. Consider bringing the neighbors a little something, even if you don't already know them. "Hi, we're the Roses. I'm Mary, and this is Yoko. We live in the red house across the street. We made you some cookies. Bye."

Sleep Walk. Put on a jacket over your pajamas, grab a flashlight, and take a walk around the block in the dark. Talk about the shadows, smells, and sounds. It's a good way to open up the senses. (Everything seems different at night.) Focus on what's interesting rather than what seems scary. An alternative to walking might be an after-dark drive to a special place. This activity began as a way to soothe Annie, who was having trouble getting to sleep. Later, it became a favorite way for a mom and her daughter to share a special time.

★ MAKE A MAP ★

Making a simple map of the neighborhood helps a little one understand how her world fits together. It's also great practice for turning real things into abstract symbols, then decoding the symbols to "read" the map later on.

Make a Map. Supply your child with a paper pad and a marker.

1. Go out for a walk. Start the map by drawing the door where you left.
2. Once outdoors ask, "What shall we choose to mark on the map? How about that tree? Let's draw that."
3. Walk farther. "What shall we pick as the next landmark? The mailbox?" (Limit the landmarks to about three.)
4. Now walk the route backward, and read the map as you go.
5. Later, back home, "read" the map.

Telling a walk can be a nice alternative to reading a story. Close your eyes and take a pretend walk. "What do you see? We are in front of Gran's house. OK. Then where do we go? What does it smell like?" Put in lots of details. Consider making some of them up.

★ EARTH DAY EVERY DAY ★

Earth is our home. All creatures share it. We need to take care of it by not doing anything to hurt it. Many adult rules don't make sense to children, but these do. Caring for the earth gives a child a real sense of belonging. Here are some simple rules for living on the earth and some activities to go with them.

THINK BEFORE YOU ACT

BE AS GENTLE AS POSSIBLE

Ask your child to imagine "What will happen if you squeeze the kitty?" "If you pour root beer in the fishbowl?" "If you throw rocks off the deck?" "If you take your best doll for a swim?" Start small, and eventually your kid will learn that every action creates a result and that we all must live with the results.

"Can you pick up a dandelion without losing the fluff?" "Can you pet the kitty in a way to make him purr?" "How close can you get to a pigeon without scaring her away?" "Can you walk in the woods without making a sound?" Some little ones have a talent for gentleness. Others, well, need all the reminders they can get.

LEAVE THINGS A LITTLE BETTER THAN YOU FOUND THEM

Taking care of your world doesn't stop at the front gate. Leave your beach or street a little nicer next time you go out.

1. Bring some plastic bags along on your next out-of-doors walk.

2. Explain that papers, bottles, cans, and junk not only look bad, but they also can choke or trap small animals. You can do the earth a favor by picking up junk.

3. When you find trash along the way, bag it. Do this together so you can keep an eye out for sharp or otherwise dangerous things.

RECYCLE TOGETHER. It's a perfect sorting game.

CANS   BOTTLES

SAVE ALL YOU CAN

Play the "I-wonder-how-we-could-use-this-again" game with your child. This activity checks the throw-it-in-the-trash attitude and builds a conservation consciousness. It also is a good problem-solving game. Old cans might become cages, catchers . . . (Watch out! You'll never be able to throw anything away.) You can always make art from recycled materials.

A washed-out ice cream tub could be . . .

Vanilla

a hat

a bean-tree house

Vanilla

cut to be a tunnel

Vanilla

25

★ VISIT WORK ★

Adults often disappear to a place called work. All kids know is they can't go there. But they can. Take the time to show your child around your job. The visit will help her feel more connected while you're away and make work less mysterious.

Visit Work. Choose a time when the office isn't busy. Show your child where you sit, your tools, and what you do. Introduce coworkers. Expect your child to be impressed by the unexpected—the drinking fountain or your Rolodex. P.S. Don't expect to get any work done. Take some photos.

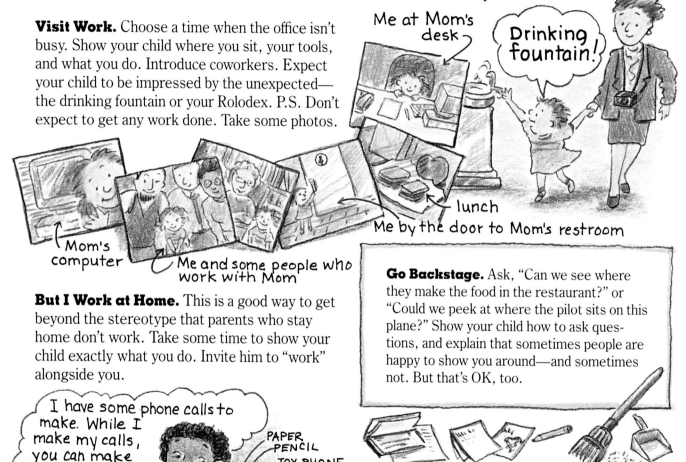

Me at Mom's desk

Drinking fountain!

Mom's computer

Me and some people who work with Mom

lunch

Me by the door to Mom's restroom

But I Work at Home. This is a good way to get beyond the stereotype that parents who stay home don't work. Take some time to show your child exactly what you do. Invite him to "work" alongside you.

I have some phone calls to make. While I make my calls, you can make yours. You can use your paper and pencil to make notes, too.

PAPER
PENCIL
TOY PHONE

Go Backstage. Ask, "Can we see where they make the food in the restaurant?" or "Could we peek at where the pilot sits on this plane?" Show your child how to ask questions, and explain that sometimes people are happy to show you around—and sometimes not. But that's OK, too.

- "This is how I do the bills." Give her some paper so she can write checks.
- "Today we shop. Let's make a list. What do we need for supper? For baby?"
- How about the wash, sweeping, the laundry? Let her tell you what needs to be done.

★ PROP STOP ★

Pretend play gives kids a way to make sense of the world, practice their social skills, and communicate their emotions. There are lots of good reasons to make room for fantasy by providing props and a place for pretend.

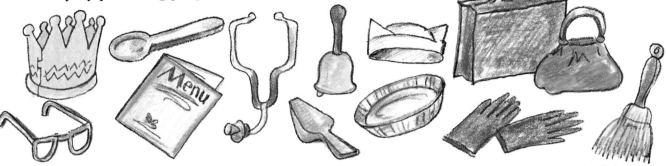

Working Hats. Children try on ideas and behaviors by pretending. After visiting your workplace, set up a dramatic play area at home so your kid can act out what he learned. Supply the props, and let fantasy take its course. Nothing transforms a kid as fast as a hat. Start with a collection of hats, and add some props and tools. Now your child is ready to "play work."

What's That Hat? Play the guess-the-job game by using hats as clues. Scout any book or magazine for working hats to guess. Begin right on this page.

DRY OATMEAL

PAPER PLATE

WHY PRETEND?
Young children need to use real objects in their pretend play, because they don't yet have the mental capacity to create everything in their minds. Having props is important. By the time kids are five or six, they can create a complete fantasy in their imaginations. Even so, having props like sticks, stones, or scarves that can represent many objects enhances their play.

Setups. Older kids may want to act out their fantasies in private, but not preschoolers. They like to play near you. Set up cooking props in the kitchen so your child can play "cooking" while you work. Give your child her own steering wheel in the car. She'll be delighted to help you drive.

The Prop Box. You can assemble a wondrous collection of props to play with from throwaways. Collect props into areas or boxes; otherwise you'll be drowning in the stuff. Rotate the boxes so some always seem new.

BOXES

CRATES

OLD SUITCASE

RESTAURANT

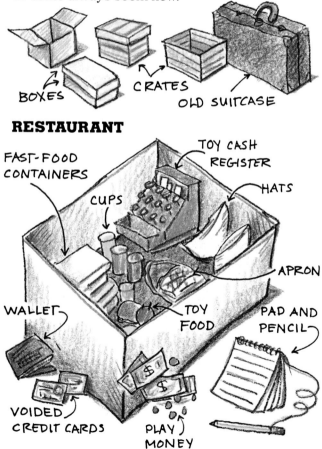

FAST-FOOD CONTAINERS

TOY CASH REGISTER

CUPS

HATS

APRON

WALLET

TOY FOOD

PAD AND PENCIL

VOIDED CREDIT CARDS

PLAY MONEY

STORE

SHELVES WITH RECYCLED CANS

TOY FRUIT

BOXES AND CONTAINERS

BASKETS

PLAY MONEY

HOUSE WITHIN A HOUSE

CARD TABLE COVERED WITH OLD SHEET

Let your kid move in and set up a home on his own.

FIX-IT SHOP. Rig up a pulley with a hook, rope, and a collection of safe tools like brushes, a rubber hammer, a ruler, and chalk (outside, of course).

OLD LUNCH BOX FOR TOOL CONTAINER

BEAM OR BRANCH

BUCKET

(RUBBER)

Other pretend favorites are camper, doctor, queen, firefighter, and police officer.

DRESS-UP CORNER. A suitcase is a good place to keep a wild collection of dress-ups.

HATS

GLITTERY SCARVES

WANDS

BELTS

SHOES

BRIDE CLOTHES

JUNK JEWELRY

A SIMPLE SCARF can be turned into all sorts of costumes. Big squares of fabric are handy for tents or togas.

ROBBER

COWBOY

BABUSHKA

NATIVE AMERICAN

PATIENT

PARENT

HOBO

CLOWN

SUPERHERO

Makeup for Boys. Lots of little boys love to put on a tutu and dance or paint their faces. It doesn't mean they are feminine; they are simply exploring a world of color and texture. Some girls love wearing pretend whiskers and Dad's old shoes. Allow both boys and girls the pleasure of decoration. By the time they are four or five, peer pressure sets in, and this brief moment of openness will be gone forever.

STICKY NOTE COSTUMES... Instant fun when you're on the go, or stuck waiting.

Adult Rules for Pretend:
1. Don't intrude. Let your child decide if you're invited into his fantasy.
2. Find a way to join in without dominating. (Remember how you hated bossy kids.) Add on to your kid's ideas if you're invited.
3. Find a way to play that you both enjoy.
4. Relax, have fun, and remember: It's play.

★ SHARING, CARING, GETTING ALONG ★

Rules are the signposts the adult world uses to herd kids into civilized behavior. Often they don't work because rules have a very different meaning for kids than for adults.

Very young kids just like to play the game. Even if they could remember the rules, they might not understand them. They don't care whether they win or lose, which makes them wonderful fun but not very reliable players.

Around two, kids begin to play together. Often this is parallel play with not much interaction. Kids begin to play in a more cooperative way about the same time as they begin inventing rules. At this stage, they have a whimsical grasp of rules; they like to change them at will and love discussing the changes.

Around seven, rules take on a new seriousness and importance. Kids like setting them up beforehand rather than making them up as they go. They can spend as much time squabbling over the rules as playing the game. Kids at this age play to win.

Kids need rules even though they resent them at times. Limits make them feel safe. Rules give them some direction for navigating in a bewildering world. One wise psychologist and working mom suggested the refrigerator rule system. It worked for her and might work for your family.

Write a few rules to live by. Enlist the whole family's input. These rules of conduct apply to everyone in the house. Keep them short. Three or four should cover it. Post them on the fridge.

This wonderful exercise is harder than it looks, so don't expect to get it right the first time. As kids grow, the rules will need to change. Here are some ideas for starters:
Hurting is not OK.
Make a mess; clean it up.
If it's not safe, don't do it.

I be the blue. The blue is always the winner.

OK. I am the green and the red. They are winners, too.

30

★ SURVIVAL SKILLS ★

One day, despite your best efforts, your child will manage to get lost. Some rules for what to do when lost will help everyone cope. Role-play them in advance so you both can practice what to do while you're in a calm state.

Basic Street Smarts. Make a set of rules for you and your child while you are out and about. Keep them simple. For instance:
1. You have to be able to see me at all times.
2. Never cross a street alone. Hold hands with a grown-up.
3. Don't pet an animal you don't know.

Name Game. A lost kid needs basic information. Play "What's my name?" at the spur of the moment until you're sure your child can clearly say his full name. Add information as his memory ability increases:
1. His first and last name.
2. Parents' first and last names.
3. Street name and number.
4. Phone number.

Lost. Play the "If-you-were-lost-here-what-would-you-do?" game to see if your kid remembers the rules you set up:
1. Stay put. Don't wander away.
2. Find someone with a uniform or someone behind a counter. Tell them you are lost.
3. Wait for Mom or Dad to find you.

Practice helps pronounciation, too.

My name is Priscilla Shaw. My house is number ten, April Road. My phone is seven seven three two four one one.

★ DEALING WITH FEELINGS ★

When your little one screams, "I hate you!," it's a good time to remember that kids feel emotions in a big way, and that they don't yet have the language to accurately describe their feelings. Give them words to explore all their feelings—love, hate, and in between.

READING TO EXPLORE FEELINGS

Characters in any storybook or video plot can open the door to a discussion about emotions. "What happened when Red Riding-Hood saw the wolf? Did you ever feel scared? What did she do about the wolf? What would you do?"

There are children's books about every feeling and situation. Ask your librarian for suggestions. Here are a few ideas:

Best Friends for Frances, Russell Hoban
No Good in Art, Miriam Cohen
Let's Be Enemies, Janice M. Udry
Love You Forever, Robert Munsch

Feeling Charades. Words are one way we communicate feelings. The look on your face (and body) is another. Pick a feeling. Act it out. Can your child guess what it is? Let your child act out a feeling. Can you guess what it is?

Feeling Cards. Use the faces on the opposite page to play the following feeling games. Or photocopy the pictures, and cut them out to make a deck of cards to play with.

Pick a Face. How is that face feeling? How do you know?

Can You Find Glad? Or sad? Or mad? Find the face that goes with the feeling.

Help children use language to sort out their feelings. For instance, when your kid throws a block across the room and says, "I hate this!," respond with feeling words:

★ WORKING IT OUT ★

"He hit me first." You know the story. Squabbles, disappointments, and problems do happen. Think of them as opportunities. Enlist your kid's problem-solving skills, step by step.

1. Explain your problem.
2. Describe your feelings. Tell what you need. (Keep this short and simple.)
3. Invite your kid to do the same. Really listen.
4. Together think of various ways to solve the problem. (Writing these down gives each idea credibility.)
5. Read the list back. Choose the solution that you think will work. Agree to test it.
6. Check back. If things still aren't working, repeat the steps. Pick a new solution to try.

Hints: It's important to let your kid participate, both to build thinking skills and to give your child a sense that problems can be worked out.
- Give your child enough time to explain his thoughts.
- Show respect for his feelings and views.
- Give your kid a choice when possible. Not the choice of whether or not to wear shoes, but "Do you want to wear the red or the blue ones?"
- Ask the experts. Encourage your child to ask others for solutions. "I don't know how to wash strawberries out of Barbie's hair. Let's call the toy store."

Let Your Fingers Do the Talking. Puppets can sometimes be a wonderful way to open a sticky discussion. Finger puppets are easy to make and might be a dramatic way to work out a problem.

But Blinko, I'm scared of a monster in the closet.

There's no monster now. I said, "Boo!"

STIFF PAPER
HOLES FOR FINGERS

THE HOLES SHOWN ARE LITTLE-KID-SIZE. MAKE BIGGER ONES FOR ADULT FINGERS.

Taking Turns. Little ones quickly learn that they must take turns or the game is up. One excellent way to learn this great life lesson is to play a game that requires turns. Lotto, Go Fish—any simple game will do.

Wait. I'll finish my turn; then it's your turn to spin.

Sharing. One mom we know says the idea of sharing is fuzzy for her four-year-old. "But the idea of 'taking turns' makes a lot more sense.

Sometimes taking turns isn't a good idea. Occasionally before a friend comes over to play, I say, 'Grace is coming. Is there anything that you don't want her to play with? If there is, give it to me, and I'll put it away until after Grace leaves.' I find this saves lots of grief."

★ REALLY WORKING ★

Even the tiniest of kids can help with household chores. Preschoolers love the feeling of importance they get by doing real jobs and the sense of pride in being a contributing part of the family. You will get a lesson in patience.

Finding jobs little ones can do can be a challenge. Take a minute to write a list of jobs your kid can handle. How about . . .

SORTING THE CLEAN SILVERWARE

It's bedtime for spoons!

STAPLING THINGS

SORTING THE RECYCLABLES

FEEDING THE FISH

One shake.

BRINGING IN THE NEWSPAPER

SWEEPING THE BACK STEPS

TEARING UP LETTUCE FOR SALAD

Today's the Day. Preschoolers are notorious for their short attention spans. Expect the same with jobs. Wearing a badge will help your kid remember what job he is to do. Make a set of badges that show different tasks. Let him choose a different job each day.

STAMP LICKER

CAN SORTER

KITTY MINDER

NEWSPAPER STACKER

PICKER-UPPER

Here's your water, Ralph!

Expect it to take longer. Overcome the urge to tear it out of his hands. Expect to do it over (while he's not looking, please) or live with lop-sided results. When your child is done, point out how brilliantly he did it. Praise is important.

I gots all the napkins folded!

Nick, you did a great job of wiping the table clean!

I need to wash the floor anyway.

★ TELLING TIME ★

A preschooler understands two times: now and not now. Don't expect your child to be able to really understand time until she is around seven or eight. Meanwhile, here are some timely ways to cope with now.

Teddy, five the clock. Time to brush your teeth! I have to go to my meeting.

Play Watch. Small children do understand the social functions of time. Give your child a wristwatch (a broken one or a toy one is fine). It's the perfect prop for exploring the social uses of time. "Oh, almost 12 o'clock." "It must be time to feed the cat." "Five . . . time to go." "Teddy, time to brush your teeth!"

Are We There Yet? This refrain can make long trips a pain. Let your kid answer this question for himself by drawing a picture with your departure point at one end and the destination at the other end. Sketch in some landmarks you'll pass (towns, rivers, the milk-shake place) along the way. Tape it to the dash. Let your child move a paper clip car along as your trip progresses.

Time Line. Children can understand sequences of events. One way of marking time is to recall what happened first, second, third. What better way than an illustrated time line of your child's own life?

There's my old piñata!

Good Timer. Little ones love the drama of watching the hands on a clock and waiting for the bell. Using a timer can also take the heat off you if you set it and say something like:
- "Nap time is over in 15 minutes, when the bell rings."
- "Two minutes and I'll be off the phone."
- "Your program will start in five minutes."

Be ready to leave in ten minutes.

OK.

Then leave. Kids learn by how you behave, not by what you say. (This won't work if you fudge—so don't start it if you don't mean it.)

"Beat the clock worked wonderfully for getting dressed, even though I kept thinking it wouldn't. My children liked the idea of dressing in less and less time. By the time they were five or six, they began to get a feel for the difference between five and ten minutes."

TIC·TIC·TIC·TIC···

No fair touching the timer!

★ CELEBRATING IT ALL ★

Little ones love the excitement of holidays. They welcome the glitter of Christmas, the wildness of Halloween, the colors of Easter eggs, the gunpowder smells of Chinese New Year, the lights of Hanukkah, and the delirious fun of a birthday. It's easy to get caught up in the glitter and shine of a holiday, focus on the "stuff," and forget the meaning. But holidays are more than a party.

Holidays are rituals that mark our lives. Celebrations are how we observe the cycles of our lives, births and deaths, the seasons of dark and light, and the passing of the years.

Holidays are how we remind ourselves that we belong to the earth, to our country, to our history, to our family and friends, to our spirits.

Holidays are a reason to gather family and friends. They are a day to connect and a way to reinvent belonging to a tribe or clan. Celebrations are how we pass the sense of what is important along to the young.

Talk with your child about the meanings behind the holidays. Tell the traditions, the stories, and the lore. Little ones won't understand, not at first. But eventually they will understand that holidays are how we remember and celebrate what we value. Holidays are how we celebrate life.

★ THANKSGIVING ★

Little ones love special occasions, but don't be surprised if they don't know how to act. After all, they're new to the party business. Here are some ideas for making a traditional day fun for kids, but the rules work for any holiday.

Rehearse. Talk through what will happen on the special day so your child knows what to expect. Have a pretend dinner with props. Invite the bear family.

Does Papa Bear want to serve the turkey?

No. He is sleepy.

Find ways for your kid to join in creating the festivities. Assign jobs that will give her a sense of accomplishment. How about:

- tearing up bread for stuffing
- folding napkins
- finding fall leaves to decorate the table
- arranging Indian corn for a centerpiece
- making festive items like name cards

How about traditional HAND TURKEYS!

Trace your hand.

Draw an eye, beak, and wattle.

Cut out, and add a name.

Scale Down. Decide on fewer things to do. (Forget three kinds of pie. Make one and serve Eskimo pies to the kids.) Be flexible. Relax. Focus on the enjoyment along the way, not the product.

Lower expectations, and turn up your sense of humor. Holidays can overwhelm kids (not to mention adults). New things can be scary. Little ones are often nervous around older relatives and suspicious of new foods. Serve some foods kids love.

Ooh, you're so cute!

Tell stories about the holidays when you were a kid. Pass on details of the special days and ways of your family traditions. Create some new ones, too.

★ A HAPPY VALENTINE ★

Why wait for February to make valentines for those you love? Any time is a good time to learn about expressing and sending love.

Make a Valentine.

Cut a heart from lightweight cardboard. Punch it with random holes. Invite your child to sew up the holes with ribbons or colored yarn. Add stickers or other items. Write a message on the back. Slide the heart into an envelope. You write the address, but invite your child to lick the stamps and seal the envelope.

> Niko, what should we say to Grandpa?

> Hi, Grandpa. I gots a puppy named Alf.

NIKO

Mail It Together. Make a valentine and mail it to your own house to show your child that the mail really works.

> When does Alf get his card?

How Many Ways Can You Say "I Love You"? How to express and receive love is one of the most important things you can teach your child. Do it many ways, every day. Encourage your child to do the same.

- hugs
- kisses
- doing something special for someone
- giving a gift
- teaching your child to say "I love you" in another language

★ MOON DAY ★

Why not celebrate a new holiday at your house? It's a lovely way to widen your family's understanding and to honor the world's cultural diversity.

Moon Watching. In Japan, families make a special event of viewing the rise of the big autumn moon. Yours can, too. Check the calendar for the date of the full moon. Take a blanket and watch the eastern skyline around dusk. (The newspaper will give you the exact time for moonrise.) Sip tea and look for the man in the moon. Munch moon cookies. Just before bed, read *Good Night Moon*.

ANY CIRCLE COOKIES

THERMOSES OF TEA OR JUICE

A world of holidays crowds the calendar. Adapt a new one to your house. Here are some kid favorites from near and far. Find out more at the library:

☆ CHILDREN'S DAY — Japan: May 5, a day for wishing children happiness

☆ FASTELAVN — Denmark: February 24. Kids poke their parents awake with sticks.

☆ BLESSING OF THE ANIMALS — Mexico: January 17

☆ KWANZAA — USA: December 26 to January 1, celebrating African-American traditions

☆ GUY FAWKES DAY — England: November 5, a rowdy remembering of a favorite villain

☆ MAY DAY — Britain: May 1, a flower festival to welcome spring

PLUS Cat Day in Belgium, the Singapore Kite Festival, the Yam Festival in Ghana, Saint Patrick's Day, to name a few more . . .

★ GIVE-AND-TAKE ★

Every gift has a giver and a receiver. Little ones deserve to know both the fun of receiving and the joy of giving. Here are some small ways to start.

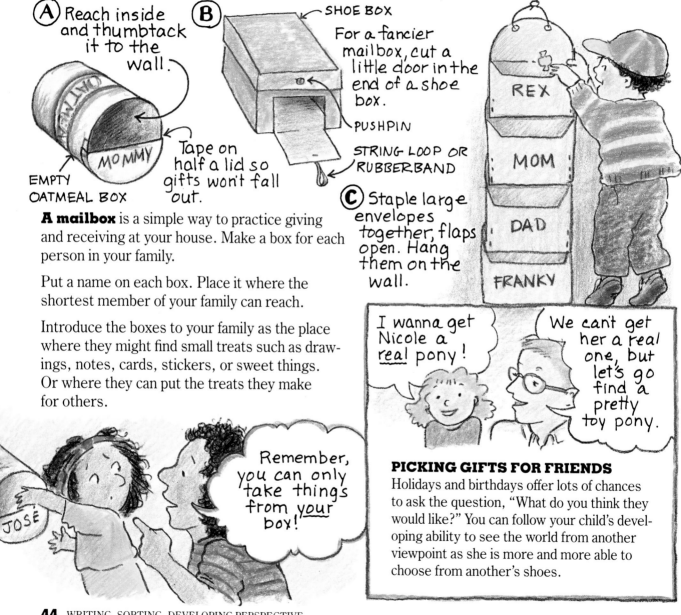

(A) Reach inside and thumbtack it to the wall.

MOMMY

EMPTY OATMEAL BOX

Tape on half a lid so gifts won't fall out.

(B) SHOE BOX

For a fancier mailbox, cut a little door in the end of a shoe box.

PUSHPIN

STRING LOOP OR RUBBERBAND

(C) Staple large envelopes together, flaps open. Hang them on the wall.

REX
MOM
DAD
FRANKY

A mailbox is a simple way to practice giving and receiving at your house. Make a box for each person in your family.

Put a name on each box. Place it where the shortest member of your family can reach.

Introduce the boxes to your family as the place where they might find small treats such as drawings, notes, cards, stickers, or sweet things. Or where they can put the treats they make for others.

JOSÉ

Remember, you can only take things from your box!

I wanna get Nicole a <u>real</u> pony!

We can't get her a real one, but let's go find a pretty toy pony.

PICKING GIFTS FOR FRIENDS
Holidays and birthdays offer lots of chances to ask the question, "What do you think they would like?" You can follow your child's developing ability to see the world from another viewpoint as she is more and more able to choose from another's shoes.

★ LITTLE GIFTS ★

Little ones usually feel enormously proud of whatever they make. Here are some presents for your kid to try on his own or with a little start-up help.

DRAWINGS

VASE
A toothpaste lid filled with tiny flowers or leaves.

GLITTER SHAPES
Cut out shapes from Styrofoam meat trays. GLUE
Glue two together if you want.
Add glue and glitter to tops.

CARDS

LETTERS

WRAPPING PAPER

RED FROSTING

SPECIAL COOKIES
Store-bought plain, with kid-added frosting or candies

GLITTER HANDS
Trace hands, cut them out, and glue onto black paper. Add glue and glitter.

SHELL BOXES
Glue on real shells or dry pasta.

YARN-WRAPPED STARS
You cut them out of Styrofoam trays or cardboard; your child wraps them.

Mama will love this cookie!

MAMA

Give out **FOIL SQUARES** for wrapping...

or for their own unique gift ideas.
FOIL JEWELS
FOIL BRACELET AND RING

★ HALF BIRTHDAY ★

Birthdays are very special days. They are a way to celebrate the great strides your child is making and a way for parents to say, "I love to watch how you are growing." Unfortunately, they only come once a year, unless . . .

Celebrate a Half Birthday. Throw a party just as you would on any birthday, only plan the party for 182 days from the real birthday. You might:

1. Invite half the usual number of friends.
2. Serve half a cake.
3. Decorate it with half candles.
4. Pour half glasses of milk.
5. Sing half the birthday song.
6. Give half presents, such as one shoe (the other to be found later), a game with half the parts, or half a box of crayons.

Happy birthday to you, happy birthday to you, happy.

Here's my half present to you!

Hey, that looks like only half a biscuit.

HALF PRESENTS COULD BE . . .

BALL AND JACKS

SOCKS ONE THE OTHER

Scaled-Down Version. If a full-blown party isn't in the cards, make it simpler. Serve cupcakes, sing half the birthday song, and let your child stay up half an hour past his usual bedtime.

This party was so successful that one mom we know is considering a three-quarters birthday. More magic and more math is in store.

★ PET PARTY ★

Francine and Dave are cats. The live with Lucy, who is four. When Lucy learned the cats were about to be seven, she thought they should have a party. So they did. Lucy was in charge of all the party plans.

Planning the party is what this activity is about. If there are no pets at your house, invite a doll or bear as the honored guest. Let your little one direct as much as possible, deciding what will happen and how to get ready for it.

1. Who is invited? Do we make invitations or call the guests?
2. When is the party?
3. Will there be food? What kind? Lucy knew that Fran wanted a cake, but that she probably wouldn't eat it. What would she eat? Tuna. So Fran got tuna and whipped cream.

4. Presents? Lucy knew the place to go was the pet store. She picked out a water dish and some catnip toys. These were a wild success, although the cats needed help getting them unwrapped.
5. Party hats? Lucy thought this was a good idea, until Mom reminded her that cats don't like getting dressed up. They skipped the hats.

Lucy had more fun celebrating the cats' birthday than her mom's. Probably because she had more control, and cats never worry about the mess.

DEVELOPING PERSPECTIVE, PLANNING, CREATIVITY **47**

★ INDEX ★

Use this index to quickly find an appropriate activity for wherever you happen to be. Check the Contents at the front of this book for a complete activity list.